a collection of
poetry

Melissa

2015 - Reboot Version

Bernard Gadd

HALLARD PRESS

Published by Hallard Press
Papakura
Aotearoa/New Zealand
2015

ISBN-13: 978-0-9876529-9-7

Cover and inside design Hallard Press.
Front Cover photography - Stock footage provided by dusk (ice)
and stockbroker (model)/Pond5.com
Back Cover photography - Stock footage provided by dusk (ice)
and stockbroker (model) and kozodyorovsa (ice texture on
model)/Pond5.com
The person depicted is a model and their likeness is being used for
illustrative purposes only.
Cover Font: EpoXYhistoRy by Segments Design/Last Soundtrack

Contents

Aknowledgements   7

Foreward by Hone Tuwhare   9

Fragments on Te Whiti   11

Verisons of the Kananga   19

Further Verisons of the Kananga   23

Schoolroom   27

To You, Taitamahine   29

Verses from an Alaskan Idyll   31

In Absence   39

Melissa   41

Two Writers   51

Sun Tamer   55

Maui Words   57

Sir   59

A Burying   67

Backward   69

Glossary and Notes   71

Other Voices   72

About the author   73

Acknowledgements

Melissa was first printed in 1980 by what was then known as Hillary Press, in a co-operative effort of staff and students of Hillary College, Otara, as a project to teach the crafts of writing, laying out a book, printing it and then marketing and selling.

It is republished now on its 35th anniversary in 2015 and rebooted with new format, new font and bonus material.

Some of the verses have also over the years been published separately in:

Islands

Landfall

Mate

The Listener

The Post-Primary Teachers' Association Journal

Poems of Today: An Anthology

Samvedana

Writers Magazine

Of Ionian Pipi Beaches

I've never before been entrusted by a friend to write a foreward for a book, and when Bernie asked, I thought, dear Chairman Mao, is this man serious?

When I opened Bernie's manuscript of poems, I saw a couple I already knew. Compelling? Well, they were like two arms beckoning: come in. It was all right, too, meeting the rest of the 'family', each reacting to me differently and sometimes thinly with a warming indifference: multi-coloured, and fathered I think, by roguish fellows. The kids at least would share a common mother uncommonly first-rate, and with a claimant sky-canoe stretching wings way back to some depleted Ionian pipi-beach.

But here's a finger-tickling line title for you: 'on intercourse being forbidden during harvest', this is followed by a low key three line throw-away Rabelais: the crease-lines of my grin deepen.

And lo lo lo: the marvel of it! Love poems sensuous growing crisply and well on that tempting apple tree igloo-ed in an Alaskan setting – for chrissake! Each poem a splintered, hard-edged, re-defined ache.

Taitamahine and the poems to Melissa confirm/affirm an everlasting sweet-ache in all men.

There are thirty-three poems in all; in execution mannerly and well-wrought. Here's an even strength spread well, and with a certain high-stepping elegance and fire as close and precise as may be to a Spanish dance.

fairburn, baxter, got stoned on the head
mason's ashes have turned blood red ...

Hone Tuwhare
Dunedin, 13 Maehe, 1979

Fragments on Te Whiti

I

Titokowaru ate the flesh of men;
his niu the earth to heaven joined.
Fifty bayonets blazed in bracken –
Rangi's tiers again are void.

II

Te Whiti speaks

there'll be a time
when my grief
will loose words
like armed men
on those I love
driving them
faith ambushed
and their prophet lost.

there'll be a time
for cursing me
whose promises you lease
at too
brief a term.

still will I christ
for you
though nails of my pain
your despair
tear me.

But I'll not die:
for you shall see
come as spring birds
slow-winged
from the far land
peace. Then
will I live
though flesh
have turned to earth.

III

*The taking of Parihaka
(5 November 1881)*

loaves of new
bread were ready
to be broken children
skipped and sang

gunners on the hilltop
lowered sights
the prophets manacled
were drawn to prison

in a dray a thousand
troopers marched
high noon
gunpowder day

IV

On the steamer

(1882)

horse-power they said
but he could smell
the stench of men
oiling endless chain

V

Postscript, Joshua VI

(1886)

seven times they circle towns
shouting shouting shouting

but earth will never shake
nor sun spill from its sky
nor dead rise from the secret places

nor walls
nor towers fall
but see –
the streets are wide
and doors open

VI

Parihaka
(1970)

there's a hill
round as a skull
and a tomb
but seldom pilgrims:
our prophets live too long –
the old
have lived next door

but month on month
the bell appeals
still
to silence

VII

```
            C
T E W H I T I
            R
            I
            S
            T
```

Versions of the Kananga

he examines marriage

Te me'a ngaoi te malete
Kae ngoungata'a te ama!

though marriage lays
a steady course
the outrigger veers!

her patterns

Sungusungu oku ngau niu kehu
tenge hakahingo te 'angoha

even these
coconut leaves
plait the pattern
of my love

on intercourse being forbidden
during harvest

Te tangatupu'a nei, si'ai!
Ee aa ngaa? He'e masegho!

so much for that story!
here's a harvest
hasn't spoiled!

angry woman's kananga

Kua saki'ia i te songinga
Ngenge au ki te lolou aano

the church has 'sacked' me!
men –
my free-tuned flute
my naked tattooed thigh
will you pursue
in paths of old?

his reflection

'Aue Tetonusanga, 'ai tau
manu nei e ngaoi, ko te bai
i Ahea!

o sky god
praise for him i see
with the wide eye
of Ahea's pool

Further Versions of the Kananga

her kanaga to a long-haired man

Ko Ngango te 'ungu 'eha
Ahe te matangi mai ngango, ua.

Flesh frissons.
Wind's touch-tangle
is my far love's hair.

his kananga of boasting

Toku hata kua sopo kinai a s....
Noka ka maoeoke!

I am her night's whare.
Must we, woman, shake
to wake again
the village?

her kananga of aroha

Manga kae ake ma'au ni masi,
Noka tau kake tai toiho!

Fruits you desire – see? –
I have.
Needless to risk
high boughs' break.

his kananga of anger

Te poo 'atua
te mangiko ngua,
e 'ao ghali
tetaa poo ta'e!

Quick is the dawn
on this night
of our full moon
to shit!

School Room

it is made for oracles
this dark high echoing
cave of a room

forty children wait
but i am dumb

then
they
begin to
speak

To You, Taitamahine

foot-sure

sea-tongue rock-tongue
suck each the root of the other

dry bone cracks to clay
ice-quick

but sure at the heart
you go

earth holds
to your tread's spring

haere ra

taitamahine – the necessary parting
shall be simple
as adze stroke

my tough love
not splinter

no tears gouge
your bright grown grain

Verses from an Alaskan Idyll

strangers and lovers

1

shall we never share
a nakedness
each soul
spilling to the other?

our simplest pooled words
traitorously twist
thrust each other off

syllable by syllable
we must slow articulate
tough parameters of trust

2

love cannot blunt
the huge strangeness of us
each the totem post
deep impressed of forebears alien

their bones in our backs
their breaths licking at our lips
their nerves itching sinews
their cold striving down the mind's
                                                 marrow

god grant
love's potlatch
gift us peace enough
to tutor mutually
mastery of fear

3

i walk
a marvellous sea
the intent iris
of my love

bold my faith
shall not blink

parting (?)

1

tomorrow the whole
globe slams
between

better
to void now
                counsel tears
the slow turn
to the moment
of exact pain

we link-fleshed
watch separating dawn whet
its fruitless blade

2

light
     crushes
out
all sensing
voids –
       te kore

a darkening a blackness
breathing soughs

a spark – this is i to see – quakes
leaps
i am wheeled in brightness
light of you wells my breath
our sudden fleshes dazzle
this fresh fashioned world

nothing (not our all) able
now each to rip from each

3

hard those lodes'
long assay of us

love's proven reef at last
we break break
combers crushing at our shore

In Absence

winter-stripped the tree my thinking makes
a birch black-muscled still
twigs twisted to ice.

nakedly (ah) at the dark bole you
flesh as let of blood
chilled to tremor
nipples hardening as hail

beautiful beautiful
i weep beautiful (even feet of you
blackening in snow)
my tears drip like thaw

your lids – i am confounded – rip
of their own looking eyes rise to night us
shivering back to the
uneasement
of our long loving

Melissa

ONE

I CANNOT free them:
Every syllable of this
Still
Is
Me
Lissa.

TWO

SPOT-LIT by the stairwell glass
a stunning entrance.
My chalky heart scribbles down my face,
all that I can say, 'Am I early?'
She grins a little thinking, 'He's being the comedian
again today.'

Gleaming
moving as a freshet
through Sahelia

bright as promise of release from
g g h l
u a i a
l r p g
a c e
   O

THREE

MISS Lovelace finds Melissa hard to take.
Melissa shows her shorts an inch below her skirt.
Her purple nails at times are tipped with dirt.
She ballpoints both her krafted-paper arms,
And binds with rubber-band her bang of hair.
In temper she's a sergeant-major's mouth.

Melissa simply never has to care.

FOUR

MELISSA on horseback
has no technique.
A sack her saddle,
She claps her heels
and strains on the bit
again and again.
To gallop is all she desires.
A cowboy's Melissa.

Spare
from those lean thighs
the old horse.

FIVE

TIGHT in my terraced pa
aroha's assault
I feared: not to have left
even love
to call my own.

Yet fosse and palisade
in full blaze of day you
sapped brawlingly breached hurled
utterly
        down

SIX

PAST my head
across the fiction shelves
a mouse.
Fifteen girls scream their mothers' voices
(where might those fleas have been?).
Melissa thumps to the floor
on brazen knees.
Burns ... Shakespeare ... Christie – gone.

Our thread of logic bitten,
the words hold like rotten cheese:
Melissa has their measure, lays at elbow
A to K, and steadies hunter's patient eyes.

(The catalogue drawers quiver at a mouse tread.)

SEVEN

MELISSA, have it any way you want;
I've schooled, I think, the register of love:
father brother uncle mentor man –
let your cat's eyes close on one. Drop
this crease-faced mouse. He cannot run.

EIGHT

EVERYWHERE

i see
my own eye
stare back

please

will you not
stay
look at me
love?

NINE

THE WEDGE and mallet of my blunted voice
I drop

she's
at her perfect season
no flaws spring

her eyes
strike their truth to the soul
hard as the plunge of father
Rauparaha's pounamu mere

TEN

WHAT shall we teach Melissa?

Loving
Melissa knows
and – see? – forgives.

She tastes the inmost pith
of old syllables
she tongues with care
(Whangaparoa, Parengarenga, Te Kao.)

Ecstatic as she swims
she knows her nakedness as one
with cloud water bank
and the bone-where river sand.

What shall we teach Melissa?
Open your red, dumb mouth,
tell.

ELEVEN

THEY do not teach
who cannot love.

They have not learned
who cannot fear

the mind honed
on a cold heart.

TWELVE

APPRENTICED mechanic
Melissa will finely tune
my knocking heart,
has less than I to learn.

Her body speaks
with all it greets
in syllables that I,
bushed long
in logic's jungle,
barely apprehend.

Two Writers

mine is nature's art
slow as the tree grows
wood deliberately on wood
until the height's mark

mine is nature's too
i seed a thousand words
in the loam of my intent
than ten might surely root

(but the leaves fall all
                        in dust)

Bonus Poems

the following poems were not included
in the original version of Melissa but come from the same set
of work

Sun Tamer

scares you such
huge sun –
swell of flame
                my love?

then so – see? – i beat
beat at it
            (flesh blisters)
        beat

shrunk
        sunk
the great star of it
broken
            to the eveness
                        of days

i wait woman
do you dare
            now
my approaching?

Maui Words

I got it man (as one Maui, eh, to another):
deep in me
all worlds to fish
hauls big
as my weight can bear.
(Beauty!)
And never mind the nostrils howling corpuscles and snot.

Taniwha
whose rumbles loose
thick earth's guts – so I'll be
him,
fingers wiggling at the ihu
send this world to blazes.
(Must've hopped their sizzled soles when you
ovened under ground! –
but wait for it – ho! – the singeing.)

So I climb (this too?) climb till I roll the sun
to my speed (I think I get it).
 I won't I won't
take things ever
as they are.

Ours is the work of Te Ao Marama – true?
I'll watch or Hine Nui'll snap up
me like a rock-bottom basement bargain
at words' first sneeze!

Hey Big Brother Maui –
you think
I got it all?

Sir

1

Sir had not anticipated this
feeding to his students
piece by piece his self.
Nor the taste they seemed to have for him,
shut in and starved the way they are.
Sir feels fearfully his slow diminishing.
His spine's the last to go,
good for sharpening young teeth
like parrot beaks on cuttle bone.
Sir like a jelly-fish sprawls tides.
    And still they come!
    And still the jaws bite in!

2

The boney drum of old Sir's skull
they think, is crammed with thoughts
like muttonbirds laid down
in their own rich fat.
It's these they want. They jog
his wavering attentiveness,
they urge on him their need to have.

Sir tormented strives, searches
for the wisdom he too is sure he must
of a lifetime of schoolrooms earned.

3

Sir's heart is whittled to a nub –
all those years, and each child
                              beautiful.
Memory holds them like resin.
He marvels at his recollecting
of them all, the hopes, the pains
he felt (urgings too, white
gripped?) delight yet keen
that they'd desire anything
which he could think to teach or give.
       Ah, those memories,
         they gape and creak his old dry
                                    brain.

4

Sir Sir Sir they say
cutting short his talking
of Te Rauparaha,
the vanquisher despoiled.
What, they ask,
does it mean? Why tell
such stuff to us? Sir?
Sir? Sighingly he stumbles
    to the old
    roped paths back
    to the desert
of their youthful thoughts.

5

They die from us, the young ones.
No grip may hold them back.
Sir fossicks for a thought to
                            expiate
the darkness of his grief. His tongue
is silent as the hollow sky.
His mucousy chest wheezes
the metre of his pain.

6

Sir's guilts stir him painfully.
How hugely he has failed.
The youngster of himself
    (he dares to think it now)
is all he's ever taught.
For nothing but that youth
he's stared – and sightlessly –
his order into rooms
and rooms of lives.

A Burying

yet that depth's gape-dark irises
light's stare,

tautens sky-lid
to the lid of earth -

a blink they snap a blink
again lean bones breaking.

your (still) flesh
sealing to the marrow of their silence

words these words all mote
barely your huge

staying   .
eye

girl, no
more

no more
no more

In repost to the foreward

Just as Hone Tuwhare wrote a foreward welcoming Melissa for Bernard Gadd, so Gadd later wrote a review of a new and partly retrospective collection of poetry by his old mate Tuwhare. The collection was called Mihi and illustrated by Ralph Hotere and was produced by international publishing house Penguin..

The review was published in the magazine of Art, Culture, History & Ideas, Crosscurrent.

He Mihi Ki Hone Tuwhare
This time they've let you choose
your poems for their book. Big of them, eh.
And the cover with the heart out on its sleeve?
The typeset is – what? – Paladium. Money –
just feel it – has gone into this! What
can that mean? Gingerly I open.
These new poems – can Hone yet cut it?
Will images well to buttery moons gorged
on applause? And the old-timers, will they
have dried like tide sucked cockles?
My favourites, you'll like them, too?
Their foreword says you're socialist. Hey,
for Emperor Penguin the choice socialists lie
whitening Ultimate Thule! I sweat to prise back
the first page. Spine's not flat when Hotere
nails my stare: thick blocks dark as Te Po
on sheets light as Te Ao Marama, each tautening
a grip on the other. Yeah, Ralph, these
simplest shapes show things really as they are.
"Kia ora, Kia ora," stanzas stick fat noses
right out at me, even ones I don't know!
Words, tough as patched gang members some of them,
start lithe dances up my tongue. What can I say?
All Aotearoa bulges your skin. You've got us
down to the soft soap seeking toes that ache
across old Mother Papatuanuku. See?
Cleft-foot Trotters, sad kids, whanau
lifting Kina, foreigners seeming like family, too
rhetoric of whai-korero, *Listener*, lover,
the hard, necessitous slog of aroha. And the whole
nerve-sizzle instant in instant feel of this place.
Hone: who else will tell it like this?
Man, truly you are our song.

Glossary and Notes

Fragments on Te Whiti

Te Whiti – Taranaki religious leader, 1831-1907

Titokowaru – Taranaki war leader who led an uprising in 1868

Niu – Mast about which Pai Marire religious ceremonies took place

Rangi's tiers – Maori cosmology divides heavens into 10-12 levels

Parihaka – Village of Te Whiti and his co-prophet Tohu

Versions of the Kananga

Kananga – In their original form these are epigrammatic songs to spread gossip or news or to make a point, from the islands Rennell and Bellona, Polynesian outliers south of the Solomons.

To You, Taitamahine

taitamahine – young woman

haere ra – farewell

Verses from an Alaskan idyll

There is more – While these verses tell of the emotion of this strained relationship, there is also a short story which tells the fuller tale. It is published in the book Whanau, available in hardcopy and kindle

Other Voices

Gadd's talent, genuine and subtle, is best found in Fragments on Te Whiti. They have a strange coherency and deep appeal. I especially liked carefully understated resonances in Parihaka (1970).

Keri Hulme, famous writer

It's a delight to see someone simply get up and dance around in words.

Peter Crisp, writer and reviewer

Your Melissa poems arrived today and they have thrown me into frantic insight.

LC, friend

Thanks for these, not really for us at the moment. It rather jars in a hip kind of way – at least for me.

Editor of a prominent New Zealand literary magazine

Anyhow, the main reason I'm writing, is to ask if you might let me have two more copies to buy for presents to a couple of friends. This first edition may have sold out. I hope not quite.

Hone, poet, friend, man of exceptional soul

On Gadding and Gadling

1. (intransitive) to go out seeking pleasure, especially in an aimless manner
2. carefree adventuring, but note, not careless
3. from obsolete medieval English *gadling* a companion, from Old English *gæd* fellowship

Bernard Gadd was a prolific writer of poetry, short stories, novels and plays, an editor of anthologies and literary journals and a publisher. All this, remarkably, was in his spare time. His main focus was as a teacher, the head of English at a college where he engaged in pioneering work in the classroom - this was the genesis of his writing, when he realised there were few authors writing stories or poetry relevant to the real lives of his students, who were mainly Maori and Pasifika teenagers living in a low socio-economic area of Auckland. So he began to write stories himself, designed to encourage literacy amongst students left behind by mainstream education. He engaged them by reflecting the experiences of their own lives in contrast to the sanitised versions of family life they were fed by most media at the time. It worked, he captured their imagination and showed them the power of reading. His commitment to multi-culturalism also saw him foster a new generation of talented emerging Maori and Pacific writers and poets. He founded Hallard Press. Melissa was the first collection of his own poetry that he published.

Contact the Publisher

Thank you for buying this Hallard Press book.

We welcome feedback. You can get in touch via:

hallardpress@gmail.com

facebook.com/HallardPress

I wish
no more paper
only the living tree
and under it, you

HALLARD PRESS

www.ingramcontent.com/pod-product-compliance
Lightning Source LLC
Chambersburg PA
CBHW020602030426
42337CB00013B/1170